This Book Belongs To

_____

BABY

A Treasury for New Mothers

Edited by Susan Kiley

LOVE

Ariel Books

Andrews and McMeel

Kansas City

ISBN: 0-8362-4716-7

Library of Congress Catalog Card Number: 94-71133

CONTENTS

Congratulations! Whether you're just about to have a baby or you have just had one, you have a lot to look forward to. In the coming year, your heart will be filled with joy by smiles so big they scrunch up your baby's face, by coos and gurgles and peeps and squeaks, by the profound peacefulness of your baby's sleep, by the realization that your baby recognizes you, by the word "mama" or "dada" uttered for the first time, and by hundreds of other events, big and little, that mean so much to all new parents.

Of course, with these joys will come some concerns. What will you do if the baby gets sick? Will you love the baby enough? Will you be a good parent? Don't worry. Your child will teach you just as you teach him. Babies are remarkably resilient creatures. Hold them, feed them, love them—and soon enough you'll know what's needed to keep your baby happy and healthy.

BABY MAKES THREE

Compared to having a baby, any other major changes you've made in your life will seem small. If you thought, for example, that setting up house together dramatically changed your lives, you ain't seen nothin' yet! A quick comparison highlights your future lifestyle:

THE TWO OF YOU
Less privacy
Time together
Sleeping together
Someone to have and to hold
Someone who truly needs you
Someone who understands you without words
Shared joys
Undying love

THE THREE OF YOU

No privacy

Devoting all your time to baby

Never sleeping

Someone to have and to hold . . . and to change

Someone who truly needs you . . . for everything

Someone who doesn't understand words

Multiplied joys

Unconditional love

However, as any parent can tell you, it's all
worth it.

Sing to your baby. The soothing tones of a loving parent can transform a fretful infant into a cooing, adorable armful. Though they don't grasp the words, they cherish the melody—and the cuddling that goes with it. Never mind if you can't carry a tune—your baby will not be as critical of your vocal talents as you are.

ROCK-A-BYE BABY

Rock-a-bye baby
On the treetop;
When the wind blows,
The cradle will rock;
When the bough breaks,
The cradle will fall;
And down will come baby,
Cradle and all.

LULLABY

Lullaby, and good night,
In the sky stars are bright;
Round your head, flowers gay
Scent your slumbers till day.
Close your eyes now and rest,
May these hours be blest,
Go to sleep now and rest,
May these hours be blest.

TWINKLE, TWINKLE, LITTLE STAR

Twinkle, twinkle, little star,
How I wonder what you are,
Up above the world so high,
Like a diamond in the sky.
Twinkle, twinkle, little star,
How I wonder what you are.

HUSH, LITTLE BABY

Hush, little baby, don't say a word,
Papa's going to buy you a mockingbird;
And if that mockingbird won't sing,
Papa's going to buy you a diamond ring.

If that diamond ring turns brass,
Papa's going to buy you a looking glass.
If that looking glass gets broke,
Papa's going to buy you a billy goat.

If that billy goat won't pull,
Papa's going to buy you a cart and bull.
If that cart and bull turns over,
Papa's going to buy you a dog named Rover.

If that dog named Rover won't bark,
Papa's going to buy you a horse and cart.
If that horse and cart fall down,
You'll still be the sweetest baby in town.

HIPPITY HOP TO BED

Hippity hop to bed,
I'd rather stay up instead.
But! When Daddy says "must,"
There's nothing else, just
Hippity, hoppity,
Hippity, hoppity,
Hippity, hoppity,
Hippity, hippity, hop!
To bed!

—G. Greene and J. Hart

ALL THROUGH THE NIGHT

Sleep, my babe, lie still and slumber,
All through the night;
Guardian angels God will lend thee,
All through the night;
Soft and drowsy hours are creeping,
Hill and vale in slumber sleeping,
Mother dear her watch is keeping,
All through the night.

When the first baby laughed for the first time, the laugh broke into a thousand pieces and they all went skipping about, and that was the beginning of fairies.

—J.M. Barrie, *Peter Pan*

Children require guidance and sympathy far more than instruction.

—Anne Sullivan

Never have children, only grandchildren.

—Gore Vidal

Blessed be childhood, which brings down something of heaven into the midst of our rough earthliness.

—Henri Frédéric Amiel

An ugly baby is a very nasty object, and the prettiest is frightful when undressed.
—Queen Victoria

It sometimes happens, even in the best of families, that a baby is born. This is not necessarily cause for alarm. The important thing is to keep your wits about you and borrow some money.
—Elinor Goulding Smith

We find delight in the beauty and happiness of children that makes the heart too big for the body.
—Ralph Waldo Emerson

To nourish children and raise them against odds is in any time, any place, more valuable than to fix bolts in cars or design nuclear weapons.
—Marilyn French

We are given children to test us and make us more spiritual.
—George F. Will

God could not be everywhere, and therefore he made mothers.
—Jewish Proverb

Most mothers are instinctive philosophers.
—Harriet Beecher Stowe

How delicate the skin, how sweet the breath of children!
—Euripides

A child is fed with milk and praise.
—Mary Lamb

Motherhood is the most emotional experience of one's life. One joins a kind of women's mafia.
—Janet Suzman

You have to love your children unselfishly. That's hard. But it's the only way.
—Barbara Bush

People who say they sleep like a baby usually don't have one.
—Leo Burke

Every baby born into the world is a finer one than the last.
—Charles Dickens

Who knows the thoughts of a child?
   —Nora Perry

There never was child so lovely but his mother was glad to get him asleep.
   —Ralph Waldo Emerson

In order to influence a child, one must be careful not to be that child's parent or grandparent.
   —Don Marquis

Making the decision to have a child—it's momentous. It is to decide forever to have your heart go walking around outside your body.
   —Elizabeth Stone

Some of my best friends are children. In fact, all of my best friends are children.
—J. D. Salinger

The great high of winning Wimbledon lasts for about a week. You go down in the record books, but you don't have anything tangible to hold on to. But having a baby—there just isn't any comparison.
—Chris Evert

When I was born, I was so surprised I couldn't talk for a year and a half.
—Gracie Allen

Parents are the last people on earth who ought to have children.
—Samuel Butler

In point of fact, we are all born rude. No infant has ever appeared yet with the grace to understand how inconsiderate it is to disturb others in the middle of the night.

—Judith Martin, *Common Courtesy*

The thing that impresses me most about America is the way parents obey their children.

—Edward VIII (Duke of Windsor)

One laugh of a child will make the holiest day more sacred still.

—R. G. Ingersoll

A child's attitude toward everything is an artist's attitude.

—Willa Cather

Respect the child. Be not too much his parent.
Trespass not on his solitude.
　　　—Ralph Waldo Emerson

Even when freshly washed and relieved of all obvious confections, children tend to be sticky.
　　　—Fran Lebowitz, *Metropolitan Life*

There are 152 distinctly different ways of holding a baby—and all are right.
　　　—Heywood Broun

Of all the joys that lighten suffering earth, what joy is welcomed like a new-born child?
　　　—Caroline Norton

The only time a woman wishes she were a year older is when she is expecting a baby.
  —Mary Marsh

The secret of dealing successfully with a child is not to be its parent.
  —Mell Lazarus

The memory of having been read to is a solace one carries through adulthood. It can wash over a multitude of parental sins.
  —Kathleen Rockwell Lawrence, *The Boys I Didn't Kiss*

One of the greatest pleasures of parenthood is rediscovering the sources of joy from your own childhood and sharing them with your children. You will probably recall many of the nursery rhymes collected here. You may even want to make up your own variations, like the following:

This little horsey went to Denmark,
This little horsey went to Rome,
This little horsey went to Bangladesh,
This little horsey went to Nome,
And this little horsey went wee, wee, wee, wee,
All the way home.

This little horsey went to Bangkok,
This little horsey went to Spain,
This little horsey went to Singapore,
This little horsey went to Maine,
And this little horsey went wee, wee, wee, wee,
All the way home.

In any case, whether you stick with the classics or adapt your own, you and your child will delight in the rhythms and rhymes of nursery verse.

THIS LITTLE PIGGY

This little piggy went to market,
This little piggy stayed home,
This little piggy had roast beef,
This little piggy had none,
And this little piggy cried wee-wee-wee
All the way home.

PAT A CAKE

Pat a cake, pat a cake, baker's man
Bake me a cake as fast as you can.
Pat it and prick it, and mark it with a B,
And put it in the oven for Baby and me.

PEASE PORRIDGE HOT

Pease porridge hot,
Pease porridge cold,
Pease porridge in the pot,
Nine days old.

Some like it hot,
Some like it cold,
Some like it in the pot,
Nine days old.

HEY DIDDLE, DIDDLE

Hey diddle, diddle,
The cat and the fiddle,
The cow jumped over the moon;
The little dog laughed
To see such sport,
And the dish ran away with the spoon.

I LOVE LITTLE PUSSY

I love little pussy,
Her coat is so warm,
And if I don't hurt her
She'll do me no harm.

So I'll not pull her tail,
Nor drive her away,
But pussy and I
Very gently will play.

She shall sit by my side,
And I'll give her some food,
And pussy will love me
Because I am good.

SEESAW, MARGERY DAW

Seesaw, Margery Daw,
Jacky shall have a new master;
Jacky shall have but a penny a day,
Because he can't work any faster.

BOW-WOW, SAYS THE DOG

Bow-wow, says the dog;
Mew, mew, says the cat;
Grunt, grunt, goes the hog;
And squeak goes the rat.

Tu-whu, says the owl;
Caw, caw, says the crow;
Quack, quack, says the duck;
And what sparrows say, you know.

So, with sparrows, and owls,
With rats, and with dogs,
With ducks, and with crows,
With cats, and with hogs,

A fine song I have made,
To please you, my dear;
And if it's well sung,
'Twill be charming to hear.

THERE CAME TO MY WINDOW

There came to my window one morning in spring
A sweet little robin, she came there to sing;
The tune that she sang it was prettier far
Than any I heard on the flute or guitar.

Her wings she was spreading to soar far away,
Then resting a moment seem'd sweetly to say—
"Oh happy, how happy the world seems to be,
Awake, little girl, and be happy with me!"

THE ITSY BITSY SPIDER

The itsy bitsy spider
Climbed up the water spout,
Down came the rain
And washed the spider out.
Out came the sun
And dried up all the rain;
Now the itsy bitsy spider
Went up the spout again.

ONE, TWO, BUCKLE MY SHOE

One, two,
Buckle my shoe,
Three, four,
Shut the door,
Five, six,
Pick up sticks,
Seven, eight,
Lay them straight,
Nine, ten,
A big fat hen.

RAIN, RAIN, GO AWAY

Rain, rain, go away,
Come again another day.

IT'S RAINING, IT'S POURING

It's raining, it's pouring,
The old man is snoring;
He went to bed
And bumped his head
And couldn't get up in the morning.

Girl or Boy?

Although perhaps not as accurate as a sonogram or amniocentesis, popular wisdom holds that a baby low in the belly will be a girl, while a high-riding baby will be a boy.

The pendulum method is a popular way to predict a child's gender: Tie the mother's wedding ring to a hair drawn from her own head (or to a thread). Hold this pendulum over the mother's belly. If the ring moves back and forth, the baby will be a girl. If it circles round and round, a boy. (A variation suggests that if it turns clockwise, a daughter will be born; while if it turns counterclockwise, a son.)

Birthmarks

Four hundred years ago, a common belief was that birthmarks were caused by anything that dropped on a pregnant woman's body. The shape of the fallen object (an animal's paw, a bunch of grapes, etc.) determined the shape of the birthmark.

The Influence of the Day on a Child's Birth

Monday's child is fair of face,
Tuesday's child is full of grace,
Wednesday's child is full of woe,
Thursday's child has far to go,
Friday's child is loving and giving,
Saturday's child works hard for its living,
And a child that's born on the Sabbath day
Is blithe and bonny and good and gay.

Breech-Birth Babies

According to Scottish beliefs of a century ago,
those who came into the world feet first could
apparently cure a wide variety of ailments—sprains,
rheumatism, lumbago, and even sleepwalking—sim-
ply by treading on the afflicted body part.

Lightening Labor Pains

Around the turn of this century, in both Scotland and Greece, women in labor took care that all the locks in the house were opened to insure the baby's safe and easy passage. Similar thinking led people everywhere from Ancient Rome to England, Germany, and India to untie all knots, which were thought to hinder delivery. This prohibition against knots also applied to anyone in the birthing room who crossed their legs or interlocked their fingers.

What's in a Name?

If you have not yet chosen a name for your baby, you may want to consider the following tradition in making your decision. Among many African, Asian, and native North American peoples, naming a child after a deceased relative offers the child the protection of this ancestor's spirit or allows the ancestor to be reborn in the child.

The Proper Gifts for the Newborn Child

Bestowing symbolic gifts on a newborn continues to this day. Traditional gifts include an egg, salt, bread, a silver coin, and a match. The egg—made up of yolk, white, and shell—often symbolizes the holy trinity and the promise of rebirth. Salt provides flavor to the child's life. Bread signifies that the child will never go hungry. The coin insures future prosperity. And a match offers light to guide the child's path through the world.

Why You Should Take Care
Before Rocking an Empty Cradle

Rocking an empty cradle and pushing an empty baby carriage have long been considered actions that court more children. The absence of the baby was taken as a sign that the cradle or carriage needed to be filled. Tradition holds that either a new child would soon arrive to fill the void, or that many children would follow.

Who better than the poets to express the joy and wonder—and laughter—that fill our hearts as we watch our babies grow.

WEE BABIES

Babies short and babies tall,
Babies big and babies small,
Blue-eyed babies, babies fair,
Brown-eyed babies with lots of hair,
Babies so tiny they can't sit up,
Babies that drink from a silver cup,
Babies that coo and babies that creep,
Babies that only can eat and sleep,
Babies that laugh and babies that talk,
Babies quite big enough to walk,
Dimpled fingers and dimpled feet,
What in the world is half so sweet
As babies that jump, laugh, cry and crawl,
Eat, sleep, talk, walk, creep, coo and all,
Wee babies?
    —Eugene Field

INFANT JOY

"I have no name;
I am but two days old."
What shall I call thee?
"I happy am,
Joy is my name."
Sweet joy befall thee!

Pretty joy!
Sweet joy, but two days old.
Sweet joy I call thee;
Thou dost smile,
I sing the while;
Sweet joy befall thee!
—William Blake

Thou, straggler into loving arms,
Young climber up of knees,
When I forget thy thousand ways,
Then life and all shall cease.
—Mary Lamb

THE FIRST TOOTH

Through the house what busy joy,
Just because the infant boy
Has a tiny tooth to show!
I have got a double row,
All as white and all as small;
Yet no one cares for mine at all.
He can say but half a word,
Yet that single sound's preferred
To all the words that I can say
In the longest summer day.
He cannot walk, yet if he put
With mimic motion out his foot,
As if he thought he were advancing,
It's prized more than my best dancing.
　　　—Charles and Mary Lamb

OUR DARLING

Bounding like a football,
Kicking at the door,
Falling from the table top—
Sprawling on the floor.

Smashing cups and saucers,
Splitting Dolly's head;
Putting little pussy cat
Into baby's bed.

Building shops and houses,
Spoiling father's hat,
Hiding mother's precious keys
Underneath the mat.

Jumping on the fender,
Poking at the fire,
Dancing on his little legs—
Legs that never tire;

Making mother's heart leap
Forty times a day—
Aping everything we do
Every word we say.

Shouting, laughing, tumbling,
Roaring with a will;
Anywhere and everywhere,
Never, never still;

Present—bringing sunshine;
Absent—leaving night—
That's our precious darling,
That's our heart's delight.
       —Anonymous

The text of this book was set in
Eva Antiqua by
Snap-Haus Graphics, Dumont, NJ.

Art by Robyn Officer

Book design by Diane Stevenson